The Pragmatist's Rules for Work

Career Paths Vol. 2: Completing the Picture on Getting Ahead at Work

James Bellerjeau

A Fine Idea

Contents

Make Sure You're Not Missing Half the Formula for Success at Work

Do you want to hear the real truth of the matter? Then you must put aside wishful thinking and fantasy and focus on what works

G reetings readers! Niccolò here, writing through my trusty amanuensis James.

I suppose I should be thankful. After five hundred years' rest, I was disturbed awake by the first volume of the Career Paths series, **Thriving at Work**. It's not that James's tips for success at work are wrong. They're just *incomplete*.

If you want to succeed in your endeavors, you need more than half the formula. That's where I felt compelled to speak across the centuries. A lot has changed since I've been away. But I can already see that human nature is not one of them.

Having had even more time to think over all I've learned about people and their motivations, and considered it with care, I want to share my learnings with a new generation.

Am I pleased that at least one of my books is still being read and my name has become an adjective? Yes, of course. But I do regret people thinking following my advice means they are devious, scheming, or unscrupulous.

My goal in writing The Prince was simple pragmatism: To explain what works and why. That's also my goal with The Pragmatist's Rules for Work, with an emphasis on behaviors that work. I won't sugarcoat the lessons either.

> *Since my aim was to write something useful for anyone interested, I felt it would be appropriate to go to the real truth of the matter, not to repeat other people's fantasies.* — Machiavelli, The Prince

Because a society's success now takes the effort of many, I am writing not just to the world's Princes but to all of you. With the Pragmatist's Rules, I will complete the picture James started in Thriving at Work.

I won't tell you whether to follow James's advice or my advice or some combination of the two. Chances are, you will find yourself applying tips from both ends of the spectrum as circumstances warrant.

And if that makes you cunning, artful, and sly, it will also make you a winner.

Until next time.

Work well and win.

Chapter One

Go Ahead and Be Arrogant

Arrogance is nothing more than confidence expressed publicly. Confidence is the beginning and end of your credibility

A rrogance is nothing more than confidence expressed publicly. Confidence is the beginning and end of your credibility. And credibility drives your career.

You are always performing. Your audience is comprised of either fools or foes. The first group includes laypersons, unable to judge your substantive competence. They rely entirely on how you come across when you interact with them to judge your performance.

> *Everyone sees what you seem to be, few have experience of who you really are.* — Machiavelli, The Prince

- When you answer a question, are you hesitant, unsure, or halting? That must mean you don't know what you're talking about.

- Do you look down, hunch your shoulders, and speak under your breath? I think I'll keep looking.

- I want my counterpart to look me in the eye, stand tall, and project confidence.

Your foes include everyone you face across the negotiation table. The numbers of your foes include all those you're competing against. You're competing not just with other experts, but with everyone who wants to come across as competent.

Some of your foes are positioned to know when you're bluffing. This could be because they're also subject matter experts or because they're prone to bluff themselves.

But tell yourself they'll never figure it out from your demeanor. And if you maintain absolute consistency in your confidence, no one else will see through your façade.

Here are some examples to inspire us

Here's how James says he heard former GE General Counsel Ben Heineman describe his approach:

Often wrong, never in doubt.

That's the right attitude. Although I suspect Mr. Heineman was only pretending to be humble in saying he was often wrong. His confidence comes through clearly. Even though he knows he sometimes will be wrong, he projects confidence absolutely. Follow his example.

I can give you further inspiration from my side of the mortal plane. A friend with the unfortunate nickname Dizzy joined us more recently. Mr. Dean explained to me how he became famous not just for his pitching but for his confidence in how well he and his brother would perform.

How can you not love his bravado:

It ain't bragging if you can do it.

And that's even more right. The **single best way to be confident is to be competent**. To know you can back up your words with action.

This takes us to the wisdom in James's earlier advice to show Ambition in the sense that you desire to get better. You should always be working to improve. This will give you the skills to back up your words with actions.

In summary

Do the hard work necessary to develop competence in core areas of expertise. Leverage that competence to get used to feeling confident. Then expand on the situations where you feel confident.

Be clear in your mind that you are a winner, you know what you're talking about, and you will succeed. Project your confidence like a standing wave around you and watch the dominoes fall.

Until next time.

Work well and win.

Chapter Two

It Is Sometimes Necessary To Be a Bastard

To recognize what each situation demands is simple survival. Help others when it helps you. You will both benefit

B e a bastard. To know the wisdom of this statement is to ask yourself two questions:

- How much do you think other people truly care about your success?

- And, perhaps as illuminating, how much do you care about others' success?

I am sure you can think of many people who've supported you in your career. Bosses, mentors, and colleagues who gave you precious assistance when you needed it. But did any of them do so at a cost to themselves?

Now consider your answer to the second question. Doubtless, you can think of many times when you aided a colleague. Perhaps you count as one of your core values helping others to succeed. All well and good.

How does your behavior hold up when you are forced to choose between helping others and advancing your own interests? It is easy to help others when you are in fact helping yourself, or at least not incurring any sacrifice.

To recognize what each situation demands is simple survival. Help others when it helps you. You will both benefit. But to help another when it advances them at your cost is a fool's game.

If you want to advance your career, that means taking advantage of opportunities that may appear but rarely. You must be able to tell the difference between altruism and sacrifice and adapt your behavior accordingly:

> *What matters is that he [a ruler] has the sort of character that can change tack as luck and circumstances demand ... stick to the good if he can but know how to be bad when the occasion demands.* — Machiavelli, The Prince

When you give heed to your own interests, people may think of you as selfish. When you put your interests ahead of those who would jump ahead of you, they might even call you a bastard.

But wouldn't you rather dispense your own assistance from a position of power than rely upon the goodwill of others that can evaporate when it suits them?

How does this play out in practice?

Your colleagues in competition with you will not hesitate to advance their interests when they can. Management will test your motivation and question your ability. Even when you demonstrate your ambition, they may not credit your capability.

Your task is to demonstrate an unwavering conviction that others' faith in you is well-placed:

> *The general public's mood will swing. It's easy to convince people of something, but hard to keep them convinced. So when they stop believing in you, you must be in a position to force them to believe.* — Machiavelli, The Prince

James's earlier advice was to have Belief in the sense that you cultivate the self-confidence that you will succeed. This is excellent advice. Today's lesson just takes the natural step further — you must also *act* in accordance with your belief.

If you believe you are not only up to the job, but the best person for the role, then it is appropriate for you to do whatever is necessary to keep advancing towards the role and then staying in the role.

In summary

By all means, help others whenever you can. Develop a reputation as a caring, generous mentor. But make sure that your help never comes at the cost of your own advancement.

Remember that no one will look out for your interests as well as you. Even if they would be so foolish as to sacrifice for you, they don't know your inner desires and fears.

You can navigate these waters safely, provided you recognize the truth of where you are sailing. You are the captain of your ship. Being a responsible captain means taking the hard decisions as needed.

Getting the ship safely to shore means applying a fair, but disciplined hand. Court martials, keelhauls, and even walking the plank are all part of the captain's duty.

Just remember whose interests come first, and you will succeed.

Until next time.

Work well and win.

Chapter Three

Take Credit Whenever You Can

When your actions have contributed to the outcome, you may always take credit and must do so

W ho exactly will tell you that it is selfish to take credit for your work? That we should play nicely with one another and leave our egos aside?

Chances are these subversive ideas come from someone who has already ascended to a position of power and wishes to remain there. Either that or someone who sees little prospect of advancement by their own efforts and wants to ride your coattails.

Let me explain some simple truths about how the world works. These truths make clear why it is appropriate to take credit in every circumstance where the opportunity presents itself.

First, consider the role of chance in many outcomes at work. We plan, we toil, and we respond to unpredictable circumstances. How likely is it that anyone foresees everything that occurs?

> *Luck decides the half of what we do, but it leaves the other half, more or less, to us.* — Machiavelli, The Prince

When no one has a clear idea of what is happening at the time and no one has perfect insight into what results their actions might bring, you must take credit for everything that goes your way.

The logic of this conclusion is inescapable. If you are humble, if you downplay that your actions had the intended consequences, you will not be considered a hero. No, people will not even realize that you are being selfless:

> *It would be nice to be seen as generous. All the same, being generous just to be seen to be so will damage you. Generosity practiced out of real good will, as it should be, risks passing unnoticed.* — Machiavelli, The Prince

There is something even worse than seeing your own selflessness go unrecognized. Consider that while the outcomes of our actions are unpredictable, the behavior of others is not.

The second truth I want you to see is that your colleagues will seek to take credit for lucky outcomes. Into the space left by your generosity, a person practicing the lessons from last time (Bastard) will happily step in.

Be careful, though; there are dangers in taking credit

Some lessons flow from simple rules, whose application we can be confident will always give the desired result. Being aware of one's self-interest and acting accordingly is one such rule.

The rules around taking credit are not so simple. Here is what we can say with certainty.

- When your actions have contributed to the outcome, you may always take credit and must do so

- When luck has played a role in the outcome, you must be vigilant for the opportunity to take credit, especially when others will do so

- When others' actions are responsible for the outcome, you may not claim credit for their work, at least not directly. You will not only make an enemy but cause others to mistrust you

Even though another's deeds may have carried the day, you still have opportunities to swing admiration in your favor. This is particularly so when you can take responsibility for any part of the composition of the team or their decisions:

> *The quality of the ministers will reflect [the ruler's] good sense or lack of it and give people their first impression of the way the ruler's mind is working. If his ministers are capable and loyal, people will always reckon a ruler astute, because he was able to recognize their ability and command their loyalty.* — Machiavelli, The Prince

You want to be seen assembling a high-performing team and directing their efforts towards the desired outcome. When it is clear you were the organizing force, then you can take *indirect* credit by lavishly praising the work of the team. After all, it was you who brought them together and created the conditions for their good work.

And if you keep the team working well by instilling in them the desire to cooperate, by telling them that it is selfish to take credit for individual efforts, you have learned this week's lesson well.

In summary

James's earlier advice was to practice Continuous Improvement. I agree that slow and steady progress will advance you unstoppably towards your goals.

One of the best ways to capitalize on that progress is to make sure others recognize what you've done. This is so whether success comes through blind luck, through your own actions, or that of others.

Take credit where credit is due and remember that you always deserve to take credit.

Until next time.

Work well and win.

Chapter Four

Demand What You Deserve

The most enlightened boss and the most supportive work environment will miss out on chances to meet your needs. Unless you demand it

I n our previous lesson about the importance of taking Credit for successful outcomes, I noted that luck often plays a role in life. Today I want to expand on this idea because understanding how to work with luck is vital for any leader.

Average performers think luck is responsible for people's success. This is not so. Luck randomly and variably presents opportunities. It is always up to the leader to first recognize and then capitalize on those opportunities:

> *The only part luck played was in giving them an initial opportunity: They were granted the raw material and had the chance to mold it into whatever shape they wanted. Without this opportunity their talent would have gone unused, and without their talent the opportunity would have gone begging.* — Machiavelli, The Prince

It is a combination of unpredictable circumstances (i.e., luck) and your own talent that creates successful leaders. Your task thus becomes recognizing opportunities and shaping them to your favor via the application of your abilities.

Because luck is unpredictable, you need to be alert to a wide variety of potential opportunities. This is particularly so when you consider that your workplace will thwart you as often as it helps you.

As I've noted previously, no one knows your interests as well as you do. The most enlightened boss and the most supportive work environment will thus miss out on chances to meet your needs. Unless you demand it, that is.

Here are things that you should demand, as opportunities present themselves:

- To work on projects that are important to the company

- Ways to demonstrate your skills and talents in settings where management will see them

- Tools and the time appropriate to allow you to develop your skills to become more useful and competitive

- To receive recognition for your work that reflects the value you bring

- To be paid competitively without having to use up precious bargaining power

- To be cherished, mentored, and assisted in your career

- To be promoted in ways that give rise to new opportunities.

This is a partial list to inspire you. Your demands will be as broad as your personal interests require.

Everyone is capable of helping meet your demands

You need not limit your demands to management. Indeed, you will not be successful unless you learn to make demands of peers and subordinates as well.

What demands? Respect for your time. Gratitude for your assistance. Acknowledgement of opportunities given and care in making use of them. Recognition of where common interests lie, and loyalty as a consequence.

Among everyone you interact with, you will identify a small number whose opinions matter most. This may be because they are unusually intelligent or perceptive. Or by virtue of their experience and tenure, other people in power listen to their opinions.

Make it your habit to consult with your informal counsel of advisors. No one ever said a mentor relationship had to be formal, or that assistance had to be volunteered. Having identified your cadre, you must demand their opinions:

> *The ruler should ask his ministers about everything and listen to their opinions, then make up his mind on his own, following his own criteria. In responding to these advisers, as a group or separately, he should make it clear that the more openly they speak, the more welcome their advice will be.* — Machiavelli, The Prince

The more often people around you hear your demands, the more they will become habituated to responding when called.

In summary

James's advice in Thriving at Work was to practice Diversity in our thinking. He suggested keeping an open mind to the idea you could be wrong, for example in pursuit of a better way. Here I must respectfully disagree.

There may be a better way, and perhaps your advisors will point one out to you. If you choose to change course, let it be your choice. But the way you choose to proceed is *by definition* the best way. To allow anyone to think otherwise is to invite doubt about your competence.

If you feel uncertainty, then let it be in your private thoughts. Uncertainty publicly expressed only invites mischief from ambitious people who don't know any better than you but are willing to demand a chance to try their hand.

Ayn Rand had the right sentiment when she wrote, "The question isn't who is going to let me; it's who is going to stop me."

When you demand what you want, you are also insisting that everyone go along with your demand. Otherwise, your wishes are merely a request that they can safely ignore.

Until next time.

Work well and win.

Chapter Five

The Only Expectations That Should Concern You

The people who have taken stock of their honest desires are a force to be reckoned with

P reviously we talked about how it is necessary to Demand what you want to advance at work. Today I will continue this theme by discussing how to think about expectations. We will explore how to deal with your expectations and others' expectations.

I suggest you start by examining closely your desires. What is it that you truly want? Do you want to be admired as a role model? Do you wish to be remembered as a kind, helpful person? Or do you wish to advance your career?

If your desire is to advance, then you must be realistic and pragmatic. The articles in the Pragmatist's Rules for Work describe the world as it is, not as we wish it would be. They provide guidance for working with the rules of the system to gain an advantage.

None of it will serve you well if that's not what you want. I don't know your inner thoughts and it is not necessary that I do so. What matters is that *you know them* and are honest about what you want.

Few people can stomach looking deeply at their hidden desires. Why does it embarrass us to acknowledge our ambitions? I say if you cannot be honest, even with yourself, you cannot lead.

And know this. The people who have taken stock of their honest desires are a force to be reckoned with. If they also learn the rules of the game they are playing, the only question is whether they are willing to pay the price to achieve what they want.

For this reason, you can never trust what people say about their intentions. They either do not know, because they have shied away from deep reflection, or they do know and thus cannot share the unvarnished truth:

> *Sincere words are not sweet and sweet words are not sincere.* — Tao Te Ching 81, Lao Tzu

The only thing that remains to guide you is your expectations. What do you truly want? How can you expect others to behave to get what they want? Once you acknowledge these things, you are prepared to be a sincere student in pursuit of what you want.

Be careful letting others' expectations shape your behavior

Whether stated or silent, conscious or unconscious, people have expectations of their leaders. It is necessary for you to understand those expectations, but not necessarily to live up to them. Why is that?

First and foremost, you must survive in your role. A deposed leader can do nothing for their subjects. Individuals' expectations are contradictory and unreasonable. They want everything delivered to them, but they do not wish to pay the full price. They want their leader to be all-powerful but at the same time kind and malleable.

If you cannot satisfy competing expectations, you should be aware of indulging those that will lead to your downfall:

> *If you always want to play the good man in a world where most people are not good, you'll end up badly. Hence if a ruler wants to survive, he'll have to learn to stop being good, at least when the occasion demands.* — Machiavelli, The Prince

Because people do not know what they want, they will expect unreasonable things from their leaders. Again, you are left only with your expectations to guide you. You must expect, therefore, that it will be necessary to frustrate people's expectations to deliver what you understand they need, and not what they say they want.

In summary

James's advice in Thriving at Work was to find Equanimity by learning to keep our cool when situations are getting hot. It is true that a leader must never lose their self-possession. No matter what emotions they are displaying, they have firm control over them.

This is even more important when we consider the minds of all those we are engaging with. People are either woefully unaware of their true desires, and so will hold all manner of unreasonable expectations of you. Or they are fully aware of their desires and perhaps dangerously willing to pursue them.

The only safe course for the leader is to substitute their expectations for all others and behave accordingly.

Until next time.

Work well and win.

Chapter Six

Failure Is Only Fatal to the Unprepared

People fail and projects fail. Nothing could be more obvious. You must always be looking for the dangers that lie in wait

Expect failure and plan accordingly

P reviously, we talked about how success requires us to understand our own Expectations and those of others. Today we focus our survival skills on one of work's unavoidable aspects. That is, you will encounter failures.

People fail and projects fail. Nothing could be more obvious. I saw failures aplenty in my time. A glance at the headlines makes clear that humanity's technological progress has not taught humility.

Why do people make plans assuming they will encounter ideal conditions? This only sets them up for frustration when random chance, to say nothing of deliberate sabotage, obstacles, and delays.

You must never practice naïve optimism. You must never think your project is safe. You must always be looking for the dangers that lie in wait.

> *It is in the nature of things that every time you try to avoid one danger you run into another. Good sense consists in being able to assess the dangers and choose the lesser of various evils.* — Machiavelli, The Prince

Of all my lessons, this one will be second nature to in-house counsel. Their very purpose is to raise warnings of pitfalls, to curb the unreasonable enthusiasm of foolhardy colleagues.

Dealing with your own impending failures

Never forget that we are subject to the same blindness our colleagues suffer from. Continuously ask yourself what dangers imperil your projects.

There are two principles in particular you must follow: Engage in firsthand observation and take quick action as soon as trouble rears its head.

The whole point of having teams is to amplify your potential. Many hands can do more work, and they can do so around the clock while you focus on other tasks.

But beware of the trouble that lurks in unsupervised teams. They will not see when the seeds of failure have taken root. Worse, *you* will not see when team members exercise independence in unwanted ways.

> *When you're actually there, you can see when things start going wrong and nip rebellion in the bud; when you're far away you only find out about it when it's too late.* — Machiavelli, The Prince

This does not mean you become a micromanager. You must have eyes and ears in every project, but they need not be only your eyes and ears. So long as you cultivate sources of inside information, you can be alert to signs of danger.

And you must be alert because your team will be slow to act once signs are on the ground. This is human nature: To ignore warnings, to deny reality, to pretend everything is fine. You may not indulge in these luxuries.

> *Seen in advance, trouble is easily dealt with; wait until it's on top of you and your reaction will come too late, the malaise is already irreversible. ... in its early stages it's easy to cure and hard to diagnose, but if you don't spot and treat it, as time goes by it gets easy to diagnose and hard to cure.* — Machiavelli, The Prince

People and projects fail because the world is uncertain. You will fail less when you accept the prospect of failure by being hyper-alert to its early signs.

Turning others' failures to your advantage

It is not just team members who ignore incipient failure. Team leaders do so as well.

There are two tools one can employ to help ensure another team leader is lulled into complacency until the damage has grown large. The first is to lavish praise and accentuate the positive. The second is to point out trouble brewing elsewhere.

Because we are insecure, we are easily taken in by praise. Best of all is to provide genuine praise for aspects of a project that are going well. An exceptional team member, a milestone met. There is always something positive to highlight, and focusing a manager on the positive helps them miss little failings.

Senior managers are like magpies. Always on the lookout for shiny objects (a profitable opportunity), but easily distracted by the risk of harm. You can use this utterly predictable tendency to your advantage.

Help management to focus attention away from your troubles and onto others by pointing out risks or failures in someone else's project. You are just trying to help.

The project manager will immediately get defensive, which puts management on the alert. No matter what happens, you have accomplished your objective, which is keeping the project manager distracted.

You may also profit from others' projects when they appear to be succeeding. This is because even when everything goes well in a project, it will have unintended consequences. For all the planned good a project does, it will also create inevitable friction and disruption. Isn't that failure by another name?

Call out those unintended consequences as failures. Suggest obvious ways (in hindsight) that you could have avoided them.

Never mind that your workaround would have created other problems. You are making clear that the project gave rise to new problems and so failed in key respects.

In summary

James's advice in Thriving at Work was to practice Fakery by displaying self-confidence in appropriate situations and recognizing when others are employing fakery themselves.

I endorse this advice. The common thread between what James counsels and what I write today is this: You must accurately perceive the world to master your circumstances.

Your task is not seeking to avoid failures. Rather, your task is to accept, nay embrace, that failures will occur. Here is a statement I rather like from a modern financier:

> *I think being successful is just about not making mistakes. It's not about having correct judgment. It's about avoiding incorrect judgments.* — Naval Ravikant

You must see failures forming far in advance and position yourself accordingly. Excise early on troublemakers in your own projects. Ensure that you are not harmed in a project's collapse and that your rivals are no matter how their projects fare.

Seen this way failure presents you with as many or more opportunities to shine than success.

Until next time.

Work well and win.

Chapter Seven

Go When It Suits You, Not Your Company

Your loyalty means you can be ignored because the boss needs to address the squeaky wheels

Go means knowing when to change horses

P reviously, we talked about how to avoid Failure and profit from others' failures. But what if the prospect of failure in your environment is unavoidable, no matter what your actions? Today we talk about recognizing when it is time to go, i.e., to switch jobs or change companies.

When we are intensely focused on our affairs, we can easily lose perspective. I don't mean perspective about our work but rather the bigger picture. What's going on at our company? Are its strategic prospects improving or worsening?

The analogy of the frog in slowing warming water is apt. Incremental change is powerful because it happens beneath our notice. But unless you are uncommonly lucky, chances are your company's trajectory will waver. Sometimes it will falter, and sometimes it will fall.

By their nature, some people are prone to spotting trouble. You must never be the person who is surprised by the disaster looming in your immediate environs.

Spare us their bad-luck stories; they have only themselves to blame.
In peacetime they never imagined anything could change (it's a

common shortcoming not to prepare for the storm while the weather is fair). — Machiavelli, The Prince

And you'll recognize from this advice that it's not enough to recognize the coming storm. You need to *prepare yourself* for it.

Unreciprocated loyalty makes you weak

Depending on your age, you probably think showing loyalty to your employer is a competitive advantage. And depending on your experience in the job, you'd be right.

Nothing annoys a manager more than fickle employees who view their advancement as an entitlement rather than something hard-won. At first glance, then, demonstrating your loyalty helps you advance over your disloyal peers.

This formula only works when your manager recognizes that loyalty is a two-way street. That is, employee loyalty must be explicitly rewarded: Better assignments, more pay, greater visibility, promotion opportunities, and protection from harm.

Alas, it is human nature to take what is given. Your boss focuses attention on problem areas. Your loyalty means you can be ignored because the boss needs to address the squeaky wheels.

If bosses can ignore you when times are good, how do they behave when times are bad? In particular, will they, can they, protect you from harm? Or, when the directive comes to cut headcount by 15%, will they line up heads on the chopping block?

You know the answer. Much as they might like to save their team, bosses who stick their own necks out end up with them in the noose themselves. You must be alert to signs of trouble brewing and assume the worst. The time for you to act is before your flexibility to choose is taken from you.

If you do not change direction, you may end up where you are heading. — Buddha

Sometimes a prominent failure will help you

Trouble signals danger but for the brave also opportunities. Being part of a prominent failure can greatly enhance your reputation, at least when you can claim you are not solely responsible for the failure.

Big deals bring experience, visibility, and contacts. When you can pin failure on some figurehead, you get all the benefits and none of the downside.

Not only that, no one outside the project (and even some within it) has any idea what actually happened in a failure. Thus, you can shape the narrative to your advantage. You were the hero who recognized the danger and raised the alarm. Or you were the person who averted an even worse outcome.

You are always free to change your mind and choose a different future, or a different past. — Richard Bach

In summary

James's advice in Thriving at Work was to do a Good Job in your current job and not worry about advancing to the next job. He thinks companies will recognize and reward performance.

It's clear from today's lesson I see risks to this approach. Your employer may take gross advantage of your patience and your loyalty. While you must always be seen to be doing a good job in your current job, make sure your performance also serves *your* needs.

The successful ruler is the one who adapts to changing times. — Machiavelli, The Prince

The moment you see your employer put their interests ahead of your own is the moment to put your plan to go into action.

Until next time.

Work well and win.

Chapter Eight

Hide Strategically by Highlighting What You Want Others To See

It is what you highlight, and what you hide, that creates the reality that drives your career

No one shall see the full picture but you

O bserve how people struggle on the journey to "find themselves." If our inner selves are a mystery much of the time, what are the chances that anyone has an accurate picture of others?

People will form an ever-evolving picture of you with each interaction. Knowing this yields two invaluable lessons: First, you are always on display, and second, you must consciously shape what people see.

> *You'll be held in contempt ... if you're seen as changeable, superficial, ... fearful or indecisive. So a ruler must avoid those qualities like so many stumbling blocks and act in such a way that everything he does gives an impression of greatness, spirit, seriousness and strength.* — Machiavelli, The Prince

Your inner life is irrelevant to your success as a leader. It is what others see that counts.

Never inadvertently reveal a weakness. You may refer to one to lull an unsuspecting competitor into overstepping, or to build sympathy, or even to cultivate a reputation for humility. The best weaknesses to reveal are the ones you do not possess.

When it comes to your many good qualities, they are also as you publicly display. You do not need to be courageous to take courageous acts. You need not feel decisive to make firm decisions. For every trait that your colleagues value, you must devise a method of displaying it.

> *A leader doesn't have to possess all the virtuous qualities I've mentioned, but it's absolutely imperative that he seem to possess them.* — Machiavelli, The Prince

Perceptions also apply to work product

It is not just our impressions of people that are shaped by perception. Everything about the workplace is similarly molded, including what people perceive about our performance.

The one who masters the art of unseen aggrandizement far outperforms the merely accurate reporter, regardless of their underlying performance. Indeed, because it takes more effort to perform well than it does to talk up performance, the self-promoter has an easier time advancing.

> *All warfare is based on deception.* — Sun Tzu

If your first thought upon reading these words is to question whether you are at war, know that you have already lost. For you most indisputably are. Every day you fight your boss's indifference, distraction, and clouded vision. To say nothing of your colleagues' laziness, perfidy, and incompetence.

Far from being a burdensome chore, your status reports are your singular best chance to shape your performance. No one knows the details of what you do. Thus, it is what you highlight, and what you hide, that creates the reality that drives your career.

For far less effort than working hard to outperform, you can convince others that your work product is superlative. Remember, perception creates reality. This is not just an aphorism; what people see becomes what happened.

For the same reason, performance evaluations are a precious gift. Your boss just wants to quickly come to a rating they can justify with minimal effort. Your helpful details are compelling, whether they are fanciful or complete. Hide anything unflattering, except sparing mentions for strategic gain.

In summary

James's advice in Thriving at Work was to be Happy at work and in life by cultivating a positive mindset. He thinks being happy is its own reward, regardless of what happens in your career.

Go ahead and support this approach — for everyone who is in competition with you. Let them be distracted with their inner lives that no one else can see.

In the meantime, you will advance far by focusing on the only thing that matters, which is what everyone can plainly see. What you show them.

Until next time.

Work well and win.

Chapter Nine

When To Inform on Colleagues or Keep Quiet

Do not inform about inconsequential failings. When you play this card, it must be to devastating effect such that your weakened opponent is in no position to retaliate

Inform about the failings of others

We recently talked about the primacy of perception, in the sense that reality is shaped by what people see and hear. Our lesson there is that we can shape how others perceive us.

Today's lesson is that we can also leverage this power to direct how **others are perceived**.

Our ability to shape how others are perceived is hampered by the fact that they are also actively shaping perceptions with their performance. Their self-interest and attention will almost always trump our willingness to spend time creating a competing perception.

Thus, as a matter of pragmatism, it is appropriate to let others create the basic perception about their person and performance. We can still have a dramatic impact on how a person is perceived.

This comes through patience, careful observation, and surgical precision when we do intervene. Let's discuss how to successfully shape the perceptions of others.

Everyone is hiding something

By now you accept that everyone is creating an impression of how they wish to be perceived by others. Most people focus on highlighting positive aspects of their performance. As noted, that does not concern us today.

No, what concerns us is realizing that everyone is hiding something. Not just insecurities, weakness, and other inner torment, but poor performance. No project ever goes perfectly from start to finish. The world is unpredictable and circumstances are cruel. Consequently, we all make mistakes.

Your task is to be a diligent observer of your colleagues' performance. Being helpful is ironically one of your best methods because they'll happily let you into their inner sanctum if they believe you're doing part of their work.

In the meantime, let your colleagues accentuate the positive. Just make sure that you ferret out the problems they would leave buried. The more you look, the more you will see. But only if you make it your focus.

> *If a man can't spot a problem in the making, he can't really be a wise leader.* — Machiavelli, The Prince

The foolish person thinks they can gloss over their mistakes. There are great risks in doing so. Because when a person hides a problem, they give their opponents an invaluable opportunity to weaken them.

When you tactically point out a colleague's omission, you may accomplish two objectives: You can create the perception that their performance is worse than advertised and you can leave the impression that they cannot be trusted to tell the truth.

Use your information tactically ... and sparingly

It is a dangerous business indeed to inform about others' failings. There are more ways for this to harm you than help you. But it is an invaluable tool in your arsenal, nonetheless.

The pitfalls you must avoid are these:

- You must not gain a reputation among colleagues as a snake in the garden. This means you must inform infrequently, in private or anonymously. A public denouncement is overly dramatic and almost never necessary unless it is the boss him- or herself you are toppling.

- Because they fear regime change, you never want bosses to feel your maneuvering is for personal gain. They'll rightly fear you may do the same to them as opportunity permits.

- Do not inform about inconsequential failings, because you will create lasting enmity on the part of those affected and questions about your own character. When you play this card, it must be to devastating effect such that your weakened opponent is in no position to retaliate.

Note, you will not be so foolish as to gloss over your own mistakes. You will readily see the need to preempt colleagues from informing before you can by raising your failings in a way that removes their sting.

When you raise a problem correctly, you present it most favorably — perhaps as a heroic effort to successfully avoid an even bigger problem, and certainly as a lesson learned and personal growth story.

Most importantly, a colleague who brings up the topic in an attempt to harm you will be revealed as the duplicitous opportunist they are.

In summary

James's advice in Thriving at Work was to demonstrate Integrity at all times. In this, we are in full agreement. Done correctly, your choice to inform of a colleague's failing is the ultimate demonstration of integrity.

That's because you have the company's interests at heart by wanting to ensure good business outcomes. You also have your colleague's best interests at heart. We all know learning from mistakes makes one stronger, which requires bringing those mistakes to light.

If you can convince colleagues that you are displaying integrity when informing them about the failings of others, then you will have learned today's lesson.

Until next time.

Work well and win.

Chapter Ten

Success Means Making Honest Judgments

Put loyalty before joy if you wish to have the prospect of enjoying a lengthy career and judge your colleagues accordingly

Judge others according to how their actions affect you

> *As I see it, [nobles] can be divided for the most part into two categories: either they behave in such a way as to tie themselves entirely to your destiny, or they don't.* — Machiavelli, The Prince

We reveal ourselves not by our words, which are worth little, but by our deeds. One's deeds show everything to the patient observer.

For all those in a position to help you or hurt you, you must know whose side they are on. The only choices are "with you" and "everyone else."

- You will have boosters helping you succeed who want nothing in return. Cherish them.

- Others will help you because, while they have no particular ambitions to lead, they still appreciate the advantages you can offer them. Their lack of ambition means you need not fear them, and you are happy enough to use their services.

- Beware those that help you only when they see it helps them. They display ambition that makes clear they are placing their interests before others' interests. They are just as likely to help undo your plans if they think they can get away with it and if doing so will help them advance.

Loyalty must be unconditional

It should be clear from this that the only loyalty that is valuable to you is unconditional loyalty. A person who displays loyalty only when times are good will at best vanish in dark times, and at worst will work to help bring about the dark times.

Judge your colleagues' therefore most critically, by which I mean accurately and without coloring your impressions. Look to their actions in addition to their words.

Because people hide their intentions, you will want to give them multiple opportunities to demonstrate their true colors.

- You may allow little lapses to occur, just to see who rises to the bait and seeks to turn one to their advantage.

- You must also deal with any number of legitimate crises. Who jumps to your aid when a crisis arises?

For your part, make sure that loyalty is rewarded. Whether people expect or ask for favor, they should profit handsomely when tying their fortunes to yours. They should also profit visibly, in the sense that others can see the rewards you bestow.

Apply the same lessons when you have opportunities to pledge your loyalty to those above you. Remember that your bosses are going to be judging you, and will be doing so on the basis of incomplete information. Fill in the blanks for them in a way that benefits you.

You must never hesitate or appear to be granting your loyalty grudgingly.

I am amazed to hear of people who wait some time before announcing their unwavering support for a new manager. All this does is make them look conniving compared to those who immediately make their position clear.

Even if you have mixed feelings about your boss, and you almost certainly will, no good comes of allowing uncertainty into their thoughts. They are evaluating their position before they meet the first employee. You must make sure your meeting leaves no doubt of your support.

A united team is stronger than a leader with uncertain or divided support. Ensure your team has its loyalty well-placed, and that you unstintingly place yours in your boss's camp.

In summary

James's advice in Thriving at Work was to find Joy in your work, for example by making valuable contributions, helping others, and staying true to your principles.

None of this will help you if you find yourself (or your boss) pushed out by someone who finds power before they find joy. You may be a benevolent leader, but only after you have consolidated your power into an unassailable position.

Thus, put loyalty before joy if you wish to have the prospect of enjoying a lengthy career and judge your colleagues accordingly.

Until next time.

Work well and win.

Chapter Eleven

The Kamikaze Approach to Making Progress

If you truly believe in your prospects, kindness cannot justify sacrificing your career in the name of helping others

Overcoming obstacles sometimes requires sacrifice

I would be lying if I said your career was likely to be drama-free. That you would avoid problems large and small. Not wanting to discourage you, let me tell you what good can come from adversity.

The first thing to note is that heat and pressure temper metal. If you want to know what you're made of and mold yourself into a more resilient shape, then seeing that you can survive a crisis is wonderful for one's confidence.

But we want to do more than survive. We want to thrive. A crisis offers up opportunities here too. Rather than looking at our work troubles as burdensome, see them as the vehicle they are for propelling your career.

> *There's no doubt that rulers achieve greatness by overcoming the obstacles and enemies they find in their path. So when destiny wants to make a ruler great, ... it send him enemies and prompts them to attack him.* — Machiavelli, The Prince

Dire situations may sometimes only be resolved with sacrifice. Say wrongdoing comes to the attention of authorities. A wrongdoer sometimes must be offered up as part of the settlement. When sacrifice is required, your success demands that it not be you.

One little-discussed function of a team is vital in such circumstances: The team functions to protect the boss, to take the heat, and ultimately to take the hit if one is required. You want them to do so willingly, without hesitation, in loyalty to the cause.

In today's world, few on a team are at real risk. Underlings too far down are an insufficient offering. Expatiation requires someone of responsibility and weight. A number two is good for this purpose, say a Controller to the company's CFO.

Never forget that **you** may be considered a number two to someone above you, even though you've reached the peak of your profession. What do I mean? A General Counsel might be necessary fodder when the CEO's skin is on the line. The CEO herself might fall to preserve the Chairman.

Your best path to avoiding ending up on the sacrificial table yourself is to be the one crafting the offering.

Brutality for its own sake is counterproductive

Sacrificing a colleague might seem like a doubly elegant method to secure your position. You resolve the immediate crisis, and you remove a potential rival. Resist the temptation and make this type of solution your last resort.

Nothing undermines your ability to build loyalty more than your team thinking you will sell them out. Those decisions must be rare, understood to be difficult, and taken after all other alternatives are exhausted.

> *We can hardly describe killing fellow citizens, betraying friends and living without loyalty, mercy or creed as signs of talent. Methods like that may bring you power, but not glory.* — Machiavelli, The Prince

You want the sacrificial offering to willingly step up to take the punishment. Anything less creates a potential enemy. And because such contests are now far less, shall we say, final, than they were in my day, your enemy may be able to regain power in another position.

> *Anyone who thinks that an important man will forget past grievances just because he's received some new promotion must think again.* — Machiavelli, The Prince

This is why you must be sparing in using sacrifice as a means to resolve even serious problems. Think of it as a measure of last resort and not something you turn to out of cunning or convenience.

Your takeaway

James's advice in Thriving at Work was to practice kindness in your work, both to yourself and in helping others succeed.

There is certainly a place for kindness in the modern leader's career, along both dimensions James mentions. If you truly believe in your prospects, however, kindness cannot justify sacrificing your career in the name of helping others.

When sacrifice is demanded of your organization, make sure you are left standing when the after-action tally is made.

Until next time.

Work well and win.

Chapter Twelve

How Not To Be a Loser

People mistakenly think a person's abilities or performance determine whether they will be a winner or a loser. What matters is what others in power think of you

Loser... is something that describes other people

People mistakenly think it is a person's abilities or performance that determine whether they will be a winner or a loser in life. While these are both important, they are not decisive. What matters is what others in power think of you.

When leaders have confidence in you, you will advance in your career. And when that confidence is lacking, you will find promotion difficult.

Politics gives a clear exposition of the phenomenon. Donors contribute to the campaigns of politicians they expect to win. Some part of the funding decision is based on ideology and some on malleability. But pragmatism wins the day. If your candidate does not win, your money is wasted.

Work is no different. The applicant who appears to most help management meet its needs is the one who wins the position. This is good news because it means everyone can advance if they accurately perceive what the organization requires.

But it is also a warning because it means you are only as valuable as you continue to deliver what the organization requires.

> *Men are quick to change ruler when they imagine they can improve their lot.* — Machiavelli, The Prince

You must be alert to situations that cause your interests and your organization's interests to diverge. Recently we talked about how to handle situations requiring sacrifice (Kamikaze). These are rare, especially compared to those that engender resentment or resistance.

Most of what in-house counsel does seems averse to the natural course of business, at least from the company's perspective. You slow the business with contract reviews, you impose onerous restrictions with rules and guidelines, and you prevent us from doing many things that come naturally, like exaggerating in ads or talking with competitors.

Now I know you've been gulled into thinking that positioning yourself as a "partner" to the company means that business colleagues don't resent your intrusions. You may go along with this fiction but never believe it.

No one likes limits imposed on their freedom. And they despise those who apply the chains. Don't expect gratitude, understanding, or acceptance from those you jail, no matter how slightly.

Your safety lies either in being unassailable, which is difficult to achieve in practice, or in sharing the burden as a jailor. It is not **you** that is imposing this rule, it is the executive committee, or the board of directors, or the Securities and Exchange Commission, etc.

Indeed, you find the whole exercise as tiresome and burdensome as business colleagues do. You are helping find the least restrictive way forward, despite what those bureaucrats want.

The lesson here is twofold: Recognize that most of your job creates resentment, and make sure you deflect blame for it to others. Choosing scapegoats outside your organization is best when they exist.

> *A ruler must get others to carry out policies that will provoke protest, keeping those that inspire gratitude to himself.* — Machiavelli, The Prince

Take what you must, decisively

So far, we've talked about how to avoid being the loser by first ensuring management has confidence in your abilities and then avoiding that you are associated with the negative aspects of your job.

Now we tackle a more pressing situation, which is the direct challenge. When a fight is unavoidable, and a winner and loser will be declared, you must have more than your good reputation and your principles to call upon.

You must have clear structural advantages if you expect to win. You must know which tools to choose as circumstances require. Your superior force can come from your past, person, team, or future.

> *The visionary who has armed force on his side has always won through, while unarmed even your visionary is always a loser.* — Machiavelli, The Prince

For example, let's imagine one person from a large pool will be promoted to lead the team. Among the frontrunners whom will management select and why? You made it to the finalists because of the confidence you've inspired. Now what pushes you across the finish line as the victor?

Is there some specific experience you've gained that is relevant to what the company thinks it needs? Your personal characteristics and demonstrated values (e.g. teambuilding, change management, ruthlessness)? Perhaps it is clear that you command greater loyalty among the team, and that promoting anyone else would provoke revolt. Or perhaps it's what management believes you will do in the role because your vision is compelling.

Now is not the time to be shy and let management discover your talents. Nor is this the time to merely show that you meet the specific needs of the job. Your task is to actively shape both the job specifications themselves and how management perceives the other candidates.

The best job contest is the one you've won by design, such that you are the only one who satisfies the requirements.

Your takeaway

James's advice in Thriving at Work was to make sure to learn throughout your career.

It is certainly true that work offers many learning opportunities for both your colleagues and you.

There is no better lesson for the student or teacher than seeing who repeatedly comes out on top, and who ends up relegated to being the loser.

Until next time.

Work well and win.

Chapter Thirteen

Don't Be Squeamish Applying Muscle When Needed

Be clear about what you want, understand what the cost is, and then act decisively to get what you want. I find people fail in all three areas

Muscle is something you apply as needed

You might have heard an expression like this: The meek shall inherit the earth, or All good things come to those who wait. Or perhaps you think your managers will recognize and reward good performance in time.

Nonsense. This is propaganda by those who would be leaders, intended to mislead their colleagues into giving up without a fight. If you need a slogan to remind yourself of this, take these words of someone who reached the pinnacle of his profession:

You miss 100% of the shots you don't take. — Wayne Gretzky

You never saw legendary hockey player Wayne Gretzky being meek or letting an opportunity to press advantage pass him by. That's because he understood a key lesson that's been carried down for millennia: Success comes at a cost and it only yields itself to those willing to pay the price.

> *You are unjust and insatiable if you are unwilling to pay the price for which things are sold, and would have them for nothing.... And if any instance of pain or pleasure, or glory or disgrace, is set before you, remember that now is the combat, now the Olympiad comes on, nor can it be put off. By once being defeated and giving way, proficiency is lost, or by the contrary preserved.* — Epictetus

Epictetus is right to call our challenges a battle. Only by understanding what's needed and being willing to apply the necessary muscle to the task will you emerge victorious.

Take what you must, decisively

The price for our ambitions is sometimes distasteful because it means sacrifice. In recent lessons (see Kamikaze and Loser), we talked about ensuring that when sacrifice is called for, you are the one who directs where the blade falls.

That also applies when tough decisions of all kinds must be made. The foolish shy away from hard decisions because they do not wish to be cruel. But when all your choices are bad, the cruelty lies in prolonging a bad situation.

> *Cruelty well used (if we can ever speak well of something bad) is short lived and decisive, no more than is necessary to secure your position and then stop.* — Machiavelli, The Prince

Be wary of any tendency to enjoy a tough decision. Some get giddy with power, and there is little more consequential than decisions affecting livelihoods. Besides avoiding any risk that you become cold-hearted, you must guard against any perception that you are cruel.

Get the violence over with as soon as possible; that way there'll be less time for people to taste its bitterness and they'll be less hostile. — Machiavelli, The Prince

The point is to be clear about what you want, understand what the cost is, and then act decisively to get what you want. I find people fail in all three areas.

Many people are not honest, even with themselves, about their ambitions. How then will they convince others to help them in their pursuits?

Some people acknowledge their desires but are either naïve about the costs or unwilling to pay the price. They will always lose out to those who are more clear-eyed and determined. Look to these losers to be among those most loudly complaining about fairness.

And finally, some people are unable to act decisively when the moment arises. This may mean muscling in on a project, pushing aside a competitor, or aggressively promoting yourself. Apply no more force than is necessary, but also no less.

Your takeaway

James's advice in Thriving at Work was to use motivation to propel your career. He talked about finding self-motivation to work towards intrinsic goals and values.

All fine, and I agree that self-motivation can be a primary driver of success. It is motivation married with action, however, that carries the day.

You must be willing to take actions consequent with your wishes if you hope to achieve lasting success.

Until next time.

Work well and win.

How To Look Like a Natural in All Settings

If you want to appear a naturally gifted leader, your skill lies more in surrounding yourself with the right people than it does in coming up with all the right ideas yourself

All your actions should appear natural

Nothing demoralizes a competitor more than thinking your performance comes naturally to you. You should therefore strive in everything you do to give the impression that your talents are limitless and effortless.

This appearance gives even the most formidable adversary pause. It also builds broad confidence in your abilities, which by itself in fact makes you more competent. That's because people are more inclined to follow a natural leader than one whose abilities they occasionally doubt.

> *Above all a ruler must make sure that everything he does gives people the impression that he is a great man of remarkable abilities.* — Machiavelli, The Prince

It is no small thing to appear competent in every setting and to be easy and relaxed in so doing. It takes careful study and dedicated practice.

- Will you be as comfortable conversing with the lowliest employee as you are exchanging banter with a billionaire board member?

- Can you cross any border and work effectively in any country as easily as you cross the street?

- Are you agile enough to switch from a technical discussion of protecting vital intellectual property, to a business strategy discussion on new product development, to an in-depth review of the latest regulation emanating from the fevered imagination of Brussels bureaucrats?

The leader must aspire to all this and more. Although the details will vary depending upon the company you're in, the fact that you must be broadly talented does not. There is nothing for it but hard work.

The good news is that careful observation and faithful mimicry will bring you quick results. For most settings, these skills are sufficient. That's because people see what they want to see and are prone to wishful thinking.

If you adopt the mannerisms, dress, speech patterns, and culture of a place, the people will be happy to assume you belong. Who says the shop floor or the boardroom is any different than a foreign culture? In each of them, you must learn the customs, the vocabulary, what is commonly done, and, as importantly, what is not done.

> *When a ruler occupies a state in an area that has a different language, different customs and different institutions, then things get tough.... Perhaps the most effective solution is for the ruler to go and live there himself.* — Machiavelli, The Prince

Performance should look as if it comes naturally

Again, you do not need to be supremely talented to pull this off. Let's explore if you have what it takes. The world divides itself into three kinds of people as follows:

There are actually three kinds of mind: one kind grasps things unaided, the second sees what another has grasped, and the third grasps nothing and sees nothing. — Machiavelli, The Prince

A person who grasps nothing and sees nothing can never be a leader. Even if they stumble into such a role, they will fail or be deposed almost immediately. But nor must a person be the rare genius who sees everything important by themselves. Such leaders can be powerful indeed, but if you don't count among their numbers you needn't despair.

It is merely required that you be able to quickly and accurately perceive your environment.

Can you see what is going on? Can you distinguish among conflicting suggestions which are good ideas and which are bad? And most importantly, among the good ideas, which ones have the best chances of being pragmatically implemented?

If someone is sharp enough to recognize what's right and wrong in what another man says and does, then even if he doesn't have the creativity to make policy himself, he can still see which of his minister's policies are positive and negative, encourage the goods ones and correct the bad. — Machiavelli, The Prince

Coming up with brilliant insights is hard work. It requires deep expertise, long reflection, and worldly experience. Great ideas are also typically domain-specific. That is, your policy genius in one area may not be able to contribute much in other areas.

If you want to appear a naturally gifted leader, your skill lies more in surrounding yourself with the right people than it does in coming up with all the right ideas yourself.

A ruler isn't smart because he's getting proper advice; on the contrary, it's his good sense that makes the right advice possible. — Machiavelli, The Prince

The more you have a cadre of great contributors around you, who each believe you to be supremely gifted, the easier it is to appear naturally talented to the entire organization.

And the best news is that you are tricking no one. The skills of being comfortable in any setting, of collecting good people to your side, and of identifying and selecting the best of their advice are exactly what makes for a natural leader.

Your takeaway

James's advice in Thriving at Work was to use novelty to keep from burning out. He felt that a mix of routine and new work provides sufficient stimulation to keep you motivated and engaged.

Never mind that it is a weakness to believe you must be engaged to perform well. You need only deliver results. Your inner state is entirely irrelevant unless it hinders your performance. It hinders your performance if you reveal that you feel stress.

You will feel less stress when you remember that a variety of work provides a wonderful opportunity for you to display the breadth of your talent.

If you switch with ease from subject to subject, displaying confidence and mastery in all you do, then you will be considered a natural.

Until next time.

Work well and win.

Chapter Fifteen

How Managers Ensure Employees Obey Them

Do colleagues demonstrate that they'll put your (and thus the company's) priorities ahead of their own? Or do they indicate more selfish tendencies?

Others shall obey your commands

How do you get others to do as you wish? This is a problem that has plagued leaders since the beginning of time. In the Pragmatist's Rules for Work, we explore many answers that are facets to this vital question.

We can view today's topic through two lenses — what is the extent of your capabilities, and what are the characteristics and abilities of others?

When you want the organization to bend to your will, you should first assess how much power you possess to implement changes directly. Things that you can simply insist upon, you should always implement immediately.

Doing so will make you appear decisive and effective. This will help consolidate your power and expand the areas in which you can implement further priorities.

Is the leader introducing the changes relying on his own resources, or does he depend on other people's support; that is, does he have to beg help to achieve his goals, or can he impose them. If he's begging help, he's bound to fail and will get nowhere. — Machiavelli, The Prince

When you need others' help to implement your priorities, you are at risk. In such cases, the manner of your approach is key.

For one, your counterpart should never understand that you **need** their help. You may **want** it but let them know you will find other ways to accomplish your goals without them if necessary.

And it should be clear to them that their choice not to help you voluntarily will have consequences.

What you want is what matters

Observing how colleagues react to your request for help is revealing. Pragmatically, there is the project itself that you wish to see executed. You cannot have selfish coworkers looking to their priorities if these compete with your own.

Moreover, you can also view the responses to your request for help as loyalty tests. Do colleagues demonstrate that they'll put your (and thus the company's) priorities ahead of their own? Or do they indicate more selfish tendencies?

There is one infallible way of checking a minister's credentials: when you see the man thinking more for himself than for you, when his policies are all designed to enhance his own interests, then he'll never make a good minister and you'll never be able to trust him. A minister running a state must never think of himself, only of the ruler, and should concentrate exclusively on the ruler's business. — Machiavelli, The Prince

No matter how much it appears a person is positioned to help you, do not make yourself dependent upon their assistance when you sense their motives are mixed. Otherwise, you become an agent of their success. Better to root out mixed loyalties and make an example than to let such behavior grow.

Your takeaway

James's advice in Thriving at Work was to know when to obey others and when to stifle independent judgment in favor of implementing the business decision.

Knowing how few individuals know their own minds, it is risky to ever let others' judgment take precedence over your own. Thus, you must have complete confidence in the validity of your views and your priorities.

If you've done your job correctly, management's judgment will be exactly aligned with your own. Then it is perfectly appropriate to ensure the organization obeys your (and their) wishes.

Until next time.

Work well and win.

Chapter Sixteen

Anyone Can Acquiesce but You Can Punch Above Your Weight

You must strive in your habits and performance to exceed your abilities. Punch above your weight, wherever that happens to be at this moment

Punch above your weight

I do not need to tell you that the world is hierarchical. The corridors of business are as ruthless as the floor of any jungle, in the sense that apex predators are looking to maintain their position among the constant threat of challenge from usurpers.

Your natural abilities merely determine your starting point. They are no guarantee of a good outcome, and in most cases, no hindrance that will prevent you from achieving all that you want.

What makes the distinction is how hard you are willing to work and the steps you are willing to take in pursuit of your goals.

There is an inventor and businessman I've been talking with who seems to perfectly embody what I mean. Thomas Edison demonstrated the determination that is necessary to win, first with his relentless hard work.

Our greatest weakness lies in giving up. The most certain way to succeed is always to try just one more time. — Thomas A. Edison

Mr. Edison told me about another businessman he's been observing who shows a similar understanding. This gentleman has not yet joined us, but we expect him any day now.

Motivation will almost always beat mere talent. — Norman Ralph Augustine

Mr. Augustine has it right. Talent is nice to have, but talent without motivation is useless. Whereas motivation with only average talent will take you far.

The point of all this is to say you must strive in your habits and in your performance to exceed your abilities. Punch above your weight, wherever that happens to be at this moment.

Punch others while they are down

A corollary that Mr. Edison knew well is that your success hinges on more than your effort. It also depends on the relative performance of others.

When you have rivals willing to work as hard as you and who are as talented as you, you need alternative approaches. Your choices are to co-opt them to your side or to see that they are removed from direct contention.

In general you must either pamper people or destroy them; harm them just a little and they'll hit back; harm them seriously and they won't be able to. So if you're going to do people harm, make sure you needn't worry about their reaction. — Machiavelli, The Prince

It is preferable to bring hardworking and skilled people onto your team. It is a waste to squander their abilities.

If, however, a person has set their aim at cross-purposes to your own and you cannot win them over, you have no choice but to ensure they do not outcompete you.

The way to do this is to be alert to the inevitable setbacks that occur in every business, to every person, in every project. You cannot predict when they will occur but you can be sure setbacks will occur.

Then, you must be ready to pounce.

Trumpet the failure as a personal failing. The problem is obvious in hindsight because most problems are. Say that you would have recognized it in advance, as any good manager would.

Cause the person to doubt themselves, while also giving management reason to doubt them.

Especially with a high performer, you need to hit them when they are momentarily off balance to ensure the harm from their misstep is lasting.

Your takeaway

James's advice in Thriving at Work was to know when to pray that things will work out right. We should hope that luck will find us when seeking to advance.

It seems foolishly optimistic to trust that everything will turn out fine or that luck will find us. Especially since there are ways to direct luck in our favor.

The way to do this is not to trust in anything but your abilities. Thus, you will appear far more competent than you are at any given point, even as you're growing.

You will also make sure to keep the competition down by hitting them when they're down.

Until next time.

Work well and win.

Chapter Seventeen

Quick and Wrong Is Better Than Slow and Obsolete

Indecisiveness is fatal to a leader. You would rather act quickly and be wrong than hesitate

Quick to anger, quick to decide, quick to act

You are not looking to be mercurial, although a certain reputation for unpredictability gives opponents pause.

Giving free rein to your anger is powerful because most people will not. People will be far less likely to cause you offense if they know you will fly off the handle at the slightest provocation. Thus, be quick to anger.

Similarly, in decision-making, the attitude you must cultivate is that of being quick. Indecisiveness is fatal to a leader. You would rather act quickly and be wrong than hesitate.

> *My opinion on the matter is this: it's better to be impulsive than cautious.* — Machiavelli, The Prince

The point is that between delay and action, err always on the side of movement. Being impulsive does not mean ill-considered, however. Your actions are still guided by your overall goals and the specific circumstances.

You must have the courage to act in the face of uncertainty. It is true that you could make better decisions with more information. Stopping to gather that information takes time and introduces risk.

We are not uncultured here. Just recently, I exchanged words with a poet of some renown, who had this to say.

To begin, begin. — William Wordsworth

How correct Mr. Wordsworth is. Every great outcome requires action to initiate it. And how many of them are perfectly conceived at their inception? You can correct course once you've begun, but only if you've actually started.

Thus, after making quick decisions, be quick to implement your decisions with expedient action.

Only fools pause to ask permission

Another pragmatist whose company I greatly enjoy is an American who embodies my philosophies better than most.

Well done is better than well said. — Benjamin Franklin

Mr. Franklin doled out advice in great quantities, and most of it was excellent advice. In his own life, he put his actions at the forefront. He was always about the doing of things.

We cannot control external events. But we can take advantage of the circumstances we find ourselves in, positive or negative.

Many people think bad luck ruins a leader's chances. In fact, overcoming adversity and long odds have made many a leader's reputation.

Fortune varies but men go on regardless. When their approach suits the times they're successful, and when it doesn't they're not. — Machiavelli, The Prince

If you wait until circumstances are perfect before acting, you will miss some of your greatest opportunities. Above all, act. Take control of your life by actively directing it. You will make mistakes, but you were acting like a leader.

People remember those who are visionary, even if they are wrong in a few details. No one remembers the wallflowers who are waiting for more data.

Luxuriate in others' recklessness

There is a time when you should be the very face of patience, and that is when your opponents are committing self-harm.

When you see them making rash decisions, or when trouble is brewing unseen on their project, by all means, let ill deeds marinate.

The reasons to do so are twofold. First, no one thanks you for pointing out their mistakes, even if this allows them to correct course and improve. And second, the sweetest victory is the one you don't have to fight for.

When your opponent is harming themselves, never interfere.

Your takeaway

James's advice in Thriving at Work was to find quiet in our workdays. This allows time for strategic thinking and high-priority work while allowing us to control our emotions.

I agree your best work is conceived in solitude and carried out without feeling emotion. You may display emotion as it suits your purpose, but always with control.

Be careful not to let the need for quiet deliberation delay you overlong in making decisions. A leader takes quick, decisive action. In this way, the field of battle is as you've defined it, not others.

Until next time.

Work well and win.

Chapter Eighteen

Random Events Only Hurt the Unprepared

A wise person knows that impermanence is the default in life. They are accordingly alert to where change is imminent in their surroundings

Random means don't be predictable

If you do what everyone around you does, you should expect to see results similar to theirs. That is, mediocre, average at best.

Contrast this with the unpredictable actions of the stars. They drop out of school against everyone's urging. They pursue business ventures at which others have tried and failed. They ignore conventional wisdom and forge new paths.

What they have in common is they follow paths to success only they can see, which means they walk these roads alone.

> All men want glory and wealth, but they set out to achieve these goals in different ways. Some are cautious, others impulsive; some use violence, others finesse; some are patient, others quite the opposite. And all these different approaches can be successful. — Machiavelli, The Prince

Because it was not the path but the person, those who come later seeking to emulate a winner's success inevitably fail. They note a person overcame hardship in their upbringing. This does not mean that they should rejoice in their dysfunctional family.

It was the person seeing a path only they could see that made the difference. Make sure that no one else can see the path you see, and you stand the best chance of keeping the path to yourself.

Make sure to profit from the randomness around you

If you are alert for the signs of it, you will see that we are surrounded by disruption. Some parts of the culture are always dying. Other trends fill the gaps thus created.

A few businesses present as bulwarks against challenge and change. They are rare. Most companies are staving off decay, one innovation away from being overtaken by a keen competitor.

The same is true in our lives. A person may appear to be thriving. What do we know of their inner demons and their addictions? What accident lurks just around the next bend, as sure to end their storied careers as the unseen assassin?

> *Upheaval ... always leaves the scaffolding for building further changes.* — Machiavelli, The Prince

A wise person knows that impermanence is the default in life. They are accordingly alert to where change is imminent in their surroundings.

Change presents so many opportunities! A rival falls. A vacancy opens. A treasured prize is left momentarily unattended. It is soon in your hands.

A person who fears the losses that come with change misses spotting the upside. There is always an upside. Even if you lose something, can you not profit elsewhere? Might you shape the loss to cause harm to an enemy? Can you use it to gain sympathy that you leverage into power?

Your takeaway

James's advice in Thriving at Work was to obtain enough rest to drive peak performance. He says it is the breaks that make us stronger rather than relentlessly pushing ourselves.

While he is not wrong, James's advice is dangerous. Far too many push themselves far too little and so never learn how much they can do. It is only by coming right to the brink of collapse that you not only see what you're capable of but extend your limits.

Think of it this way. Your success is affected by random events, but your effort is not one of them. You control how hard you work, and that is one of the keys to your success.

Until next time.

Work well and win.

Chapter Nineteen

Your Sense of Shame Is Holding You Back

Your colleagues would undermine you without hesitation, and indeed without thought. Why would you worry about what they think?

You must not feel shame

On your path to being a successful leader, you are subject to the whims of management above you and employees below you. You can never count on these constituents to view you or your actions rationally or fairly, because they are made up of fallible humans.

> *You can be hated just as much for the good you do as the bad, which is why, as I said before, a ruler who wants to stay in power is often forced not to be good.* — Machiavelli, The Prince

Thus, you cannot worry about what others think about you or your actions. Your focus must be entirely directed on the outcomes you seek. Your colleagues would undermine you without hesitation, and indeed without thought. Why would you worry about what they think?

A sensible leader cannot and must not keep his word if by doing so he puts himself at risk... If all men were good, this would be bad advice, but since they are a sad lot and won't be keeping their promises to you, you hardly need to keep yours to them. Anyway, a ruler will never be short of good reasons to explain away a broken promise. — Machiavelli, The Prince

Once you are in a position of power, others' opinions are more easily managed. People will want to believe your intentions are good, and so you will be able to justify unpleasantries along the way.

The crowd is won over by appearance and final results. And the world is all crowd: the dissenting few find no space as long as the majority have any grounds at all for their opinions. — Machiavelli, The Prince

Guilt people into helping you

You will have two levers with which to get people to work towards your purposes. You must use both, recognizing which persons are amenable to which lever.

The first type of person will help you without much pressure. The reasons for compliance are manifold, for example, because it's their nature to be helpful, they don't want to make waves, they see your interests are aligned with the company's, or they see self-interest in helping you, etc.

In each case, your task is to take liberal advantage of the person's character while reinforcing their belief in the valid reasons for helping you.

The second type of person will not help you, at least initially. They may in fact try to stymie your progress, either in favor of their own candidacy or another whom they support.

Assuming you win the day, your erstwhile opponents deserve special attention because they can become your most effective advocates. This requires that you publicly call out and shame their prior bad behavior. They should feel the weight of their colleagues' approbation and fear the consequences of their and your reprisal.

> *A ruler can very easily win over men who opposed him when he came to power ... They'll be forced to behave more loyally than others in that they know they have to work to offset the negative impression the ruler initially had of them. So a ruler can always get more out of such men than out of people who feel safe in his service and don't really make an effort.* — Machiavelli, The Prince

Having taken a gamble in opposing you and lost, their fear and shame make them more manipulable than the good corporate citizens whose loyalty was never in doubt.

Your takeaway

James's advice in Thriving at Work was to manage stress both in work and outside work to enable sustainable performance. He says that while some stress is helpful, most of us have unhealthy levels of stress.

It is true that too much stress can be unhealthy, but James is misguided when he says that taking breaks and resting is the key to managing stress. A better way is to avoid putting yourself in situations where stress builds up.

Your stress is a result of taking on more work than you can handle, taking responsibility for things that are not your fault, and letting others' actions affect your progress. By focusing on the root causes rather than the symptoms, you will avoid feeling stress in the first instance.

Until next time.

Work well and win.

Chapter Twenty

Terror Is a Tool Some Managers Use Well

While it is much harder to learn from others' experiences, swift and serious punishment sends a signal that penetrates the average employee's indifference

Terror: It's much safer to be feared than loved

This one of my lessons seems to be the most widely known, or at least the most quoted. I wonder how many know the true meaning, however. You do not cultivate love or fear out of regard for the individuals you interact with, but for the impact these emotions have on your effectiveness.

It is true that people will be less worried about disappointing leaders who cultivate love. The team's performance is just one factor. The more salient reason not to base your action on people's regard for you is that you hamper your own ability to make tough decisions. Tough decisions are an inevitable part of leadership.

Because life is tough, and businesses will be in tough situations, leaders need to make difficult decisions. Every employee should fear the consequences, not of their leader, but of the situation.

A leader will be associated with the decisions they make, even if the situation is not of their making. Hence comes the fear of the leader themselves.

Men are less worried about letting down someone who has made himself loved than someone who makes himself feared. — Machiavelli, The Prince

As between seeking to have employees love or fear you, you should always fall on the side that allows you to make necessary decisions without bias. If that creates fear, so be it.

Punishment serves a specific purpose

There is a time when a leader seeks to generate fear, and that's when employees have frustrated the leader's plans or themselves created a difficult situation.

We learn best what we experience directly. Thus, in such cases, the leader must express their displeasure clearly and immediately. While it is much harder to learn from others' experiences, swift and serious punishment sends a signal that penetrates the average employee's indifference.

Fear means fear of punishment, and that's something people never forget. — Machiavelli, The Prince

So long as the punishment is meted out directly in response to a wrong act, people will accept that it is harsh. Especially if they are not the recipients.

For their part, the recipient must understand that the punishment is deserved but has an origin (of their making) and an end (of the leader's choosing).

In this way, mistakes and their aftermath serve as valuable teaching moments that reinforce important lessons. What we do is serious, and mistakes have consequences. Pay attention to what you are doing and exercise care.

Your takeaway

James's advice in Thriving at Work was to take advantage of the many benefits that accrue to you when you are a team player. Interestingly, James spends a lot of time talking about how to work with dysfunctional teams.

A team that is firmly in hand, one that lives in fear of consequences should they fail to perform, can greatly magnify one's power.

So too, it can propel your career to latch onto a team that is close to the levers of power because of the people who comprise it, the tasks they perform, or both.

The one thing you never want to be is a team member who doesn't know exactly what's in it for them.

Until next time.

Work well and win.

Chapter Twenty-One

How To Respond to an Ultimatum ... and Give One

People will second-guess and criticize your decisions no matter what they are. The sensible choice is to listen only to your own counsel

Achieving your outcome is all that matters

P eople do not perceive the world clearly or objectively. They come with prior experiences and differing information, which together form preconceived notions and biases.

As a result, people judge situations more based on their foibles than they do the situations themselves. Further, because people differ widely in their experiences, you can scarcely expect unanimity of opinion about any topic.

If you attempt to please one group by pandering to one of their cherished beliefs, you may or may not succeed. For all their imperfect reasoning, people are adept at sniffing out insincerity.

Even if you please the group you targeted, you will create enemies among those who see the world differently. You may never hear of their discontent, but their resentment is real and will find ways to manifest at inopportune times.

Thus, a leader serves best when they focus exclusively on their priorities, and not what anyone potentially thinks about those priorities.

> *[A leader] mustn't be concerned about the bad reputation that comes*
> *with those negative qualities that are almost essential if he is to hold*
> *on to power. If you think about it, there'll always be something that*
> *looks morally right but would actually lead a ruler to disaster, and*
> *something else that looks wrong but will bring security and success.* —
> Machiavelli, The Prince

People will second-guess and criticize your decisions no matter what they are. The sensible choice is to develop a keen sense of what to do and why and listen only to your own counsel.

Following someone else's imperative cedes victory without a fight

I look at the Corporate Social Responsibility (CSR) and Environmental, Social, and Governance (ESG) movements and see master manipulators at work. With nothing more than high-minded words, these opportunists have inserted themselves into an established tradition of ownership and control.

Shareholders own the company. Shareholders elect directors who in turn appoint officers. This system is a model of simplicity, accountability, and direct action.

Come now the CSR and ESG activists. Some may be shareholders, which at least gives them a seat at the table to raise issues to be heard and evaluated along with all others.

Many do not even bother with the fiction of becoming part-owners. They claim authority from a higher power, that of morality or, heaven-forbid, fairness.

Never mind that it is the peak of unfairness and immorality for a "stakeholder" in nothing more than the name to demand their priorities be given precedence over those of other stakeholders or the actual owners.

Show me a leader who pays heed to such extortionists, and I will show you someone who does not know that saboteurs come in many guises. The greatest harm is done by those professing to want only good but are spending someone else's money to achieve it.

A wise leader will listen to these foes while giving every appearance of taking their concerns seriously. The goal is to understand and neutralize them, and this requires making them feel heard.

Agree with their principles all day, so long as you need change none of your existing priorities. Make flowery statements and publish glowing reports, but stay focused on the business.

To do otherwise is to give up your leadership role without a fight.

Your takeaway

James's advice in Thriving at Work was to understand the utility in your actions or the value behind everything you do. James is correct that it is necessary to regularly demonstrate your worth.

He says that you demonstrate your worth by advancing your strategy and your company's strategy. Where he goes off the rails is in suggesting that it's ever a good investment of your time to help a colleague.

I suppose you help a colleague in aiding their perception that the best use of their time is helping you. Short of this, the best way to demonstrate your worth is by making sure you deliver on your ultimatums.

Until next time.

Work well and win.

Chapter Twenty-Two

Knowing Which Role Models To Venerate Is Key

What actions do great leaders take? Not what they said after the fact, or even at the time, for manipulation and justification are always lurking when we describe our actions

Pick role models who exemplify success

We are spoiled for choice when it comes to leaders to study and emulate. It used to be that we had to troll through centuries of history to tease out applicable lessons from situations of varying relevance.

Not so today. From the case studies of the Harvard Business School to the pages of the Wall Street Journal, countless business wars are fought, won, and lost every day.

We needn't wait for the judgment of history to tell us which party emerged victorious. Stock markets rise and fall, while companies grow or stagnate and languish.

> *If you're sensible, you set out to follow a trail blazed by someone who was truly great, someone really worth imitating, so that even if you're not on the same level yourself at least you'll reflect a little of his brilliance.* — Machiavelli, The Prince

From this rich pool of exemplars, we must pick our role models. Here are two things that you can safely ignore: Complaints of coworkers who felt mistreated on a leader's rise to glory, and actions a person takes after they leave their positions.

Remember what I've said previously about people's perceptions: They're inconsistent and inaccurate. So a boss has a reputation for being harsh, mercurial, or even mean. What of it? Did they deliver results? That's a far more meaningful metric if you're trying to decide whose style to mine for lessons.

Take now the leader turned philanthropist, politician, or pundit upon leaving their business post. You may safely ignore everything this person says and does.

Even if they are giving you a first-hand account of their business days, you are foolish to listen. They likely do not know, and would less likely admit if they did, all the factors that gave rise to their performance. What they do tell will be cherry-picked and sanitized in service of presenting the image they wish to present.

That does not mean these leaders are useless to you as role models. Far from it. It's just that you must take your lessons from another source.

Study what those leaders did, not what they said

Your source of truly valuable lessons comes in this: What actions did great leaders take? Not what they said after the fact, or even at the time, for manipulation and justification are always lurking when we describe our actions.

No, simply this — what did they do in what circumstances?

> *Take as model a leader who's been much praised and admired and keep his example and achievements in mind at all times.* — Machiavelli, The Prince

You may read their biographies and hagiographies to get details of scenes and places. The salient facts making up the business case, as it were. Then apply your efforts to uncovering the key decisions that turned the tide. There will usually be just a handful of pivotal moments.

If you can learn to spot these deciding factors, you will be in a position to study what makes a few leaders great and what makes many fail. You will find that great leaders appear unconventional because they have unusually strong faith in their vision.

They let no one dissuade them from their belief, and let no mere obstacle deter them from their path. Others' doubts, public opinion, unlikely odds — these are all things standing in the way of average leaders.

Great leaders take decisive action in the face of uncountable obstacles and prevail.

Your takeaway

James's advice in Thriving at Work was to think about values in the context of work, specifically to understand how your company's values and your personal values align.

James is correct that trouble ensues when there is a mismatch between the two. Rather than selecting only companies whose values line up with your own, you can take a more direct albeit difficult approach. That is to shape your company's values to be consistent with your own.

For their part, employees regularly put pressure on companies to adopt or espouse values that may have little to do with business success. Your imposition of values will be more pragmatic, aimed at ensuring the company's success and hence your success.

Seen this way, the most exemplary leaders are those who have a core value system that is so strong they bend their organizations to conform to it.

Until next time.

Work well and win.

Chapter Twenty-Three

Spotting Weakness Allows You To Exploit It

Done correctly, pointing out a putative weakness removes a competitor from contention while allowing you to gain their trust and loyalty

Everyone has weaknesses. Find and exploit them

Weaknesses come in many forms. You will regularly encounter performance-related weaknesses, where a person lacks relevant skills or experience or is unable to bring their talents to bear as needed.

You will see others who lack the stamina to persevere when others carry on, or whose desire for comfort calls them to avoid the discomfort attendant to great deeds.

Still others who have the requisite skills and stamina flame out because they simply cannot control their emotions. They never learn that emotions may be felt and expressed, but never ungoverned, always in the service of the primary objective.

Whenever weaknesses such as these slow the progress of once high-performers, negative consequences often follow. Envy of the remaining high-flyers is the least of it. Someone who sees greatness pass them by often finds themselves entertaining dark thoughts indeed.

It is fear or hatred that makes men attack each other. — Machiavelli, The Prince

On your upward path, you must navigate these emotions with care. The first task is to simply be alert to identifying your colleagues' weaknesses before they've become derailed by them. This puts you in a position to work with and exploit the situation.

Exploiting a weakness does not mean causing harm to a co-worker. Often, you can keep them from derailing their career by pursuing paths they're unsuited for.

For example, a person who is a solid performer but doesn't have the stomach for 80-hour weeks will either take a run at leadership and burn out, or they'll be realistic about their odds and will be persuaded into a productive, but less senior role.

You can be the one to help them see how to be both valued and happy. There is no shame in this, only mutual advantage. Done correctly, pointing out a putative weakness removes a competitor from contention while allowing you to gain their trust and loyalty.

Some weaknesses are more debilitating than others. A person who isn't up to the task is in the wrong role. Short of that, you may be able to compensate for a person's weakness, for example by pairing them with someone who complements their gaps.

Your task is to be a careful observer of those around you to identify the ways in which their weaknesses will hamper them (and indirectly you). Some you can save, and others you can move, but you must know everyone's weakness.

This holds true for your weaknesses as well.

Be aware of your weaknesses

What? Did you think you uniquely were the only person to have no weaknesses? This is a dangerous delusion. You need not dwell overlong on the fact that you are imperfect, simply accept that you are and know your flaws in detail.

Once you know your flaws, you can be your own best advocate in a similar manner to how you assist your colleagues in working with their weaknesses. In the case of your failings, your task is to make sure that none prevent your further ascent.

Can you obtain further training and needed experience? Can you surround yourself with colleagues who make you strong where you're weak by inclination?

You will often have to rely on others to help you achieve your objectives. In such cases, you must be alert to whether they may act independently to thwart your aims.

> *If he's ruling by proxy [a leader will] be weaker and exposed to greater risks, since he now depends entirely on the good will of the men appointed as magistrates and they can very easily strip him of his power, particularly when times are hard, either by attacking him directly or by just not carrying out his orders.* — Machiavelli, The Prince

You can insulate yourself from attacks by those closest to you and who are aware of a key weakness. You do this by making their fortune and future intimately tied to your own. If you rise, they rise. And if you fail, they will go down with you.

Your takeaway

James's advice in Thriving at Work was to think about your worth to your company, others, and yourself.

I support James' idea that our worth to our companies and colleagues is typically higher than we first estimate. He then cautions against being too critical about ourselves, fine, or valuing ourselves too highly.

I trust it's clear you cannot value yourself too highly. Anything less than the absolute best interpretation leaves room for others to doubt you and for you to doubt yourself. That only admits a weakness, which has a way of becoming self-fulfilling.

Your worth is a function of excising and minimizing weaknesses, and compensating for those that remain. Having made this a practice, why wouldn't you double down on the idea that you are invaluable?

Until next time.

Work well and win.

Chapter Twenty-Four

When Xenophobia Works to Your Advantage

One simple tool is to stoke people's fears of change. The key is to associate bad change with unreliable leaders, and necessary change with visionary ones

Fear of foreign and different things is natural

We think of xenophobia as relating to foreign people, but it is broader than that. You can think of it this way. Any time you are seeking to introduce a change, people will resist you.

It does not matter that your new system is demonstrably superior. It does not matter that the new leader is an upgrade. All that matters is that there is a change because people inherently resist change.

You are thus at your most vulnerable when you are introducing changes. You will encounter resistance even from people who would normally support you. You will face determined action from those who are disadvantaged.

> *Nothing is harder to organize, more likely to fail, or more dangerous to see through, than the introduction of a new system of government. The person bringing in the changes will make enemies of everyone who was doing well under the old system, while the people who stand to gain from the new arrangements will not offer wholehearted*

support, partly because they are afraid of their opponents, who still have the laws on their side. — Machiavelli, The Prince

This is when all your work in building loyalty that cannot be easily withheld pays off. Because when facing significant change, there is nothing for it but to see things through, to persevere.

Properly applied, xenophobia does your work for you

Your success is partly a matter of your efforts and the efforts of those who work on your behalf. It's easy to underestimate how critical it is to understand the efforts of third parties who are working towards their aims, not yours.

They may not be direct rivals, but their project competes with yours for time and attention. Thus, your success may hinge on their project being sidelined. One simple tool is to stoke people's fears of change. When you are seeking to derail a competing project, this fear takes root most easily and with devastating effect.

> *People are naturally skeptical: no one really believes in change until they've had solid experience of it.* — Machiavelli, The Prince

You need to apply the right type of brake at the right time. Raise specific doubts about the rival's project, not about change in general. This is because a short time later, you will be asking your organization to change for your project.

> *Two men can both be cautious but with different results: one is successful and the other fails.... This depends entirely on whether their approach suits the circumstances.... This explains why people's fortunes go up and down.* — Machiavelli, The Prince

The key is to associate bad change with unreliable leaders, and necessary change with visionary ones.

Xenophobia can just as quickly derail you

The same factors that allow you to derail a rival's project make your projects vulnerable to manipulation.

Because you cannot prevent either the attempt or the circumstances in which the sabotage will play out, you must focus on your response. You must be willing to change your approach at a moment's notice.

It does not matter if your project succeeds as originally foreseen, only that you prevail in some fashion.

> *If a person has always been successful with a particular approach, he won't easily be persuaded to drop it.... If he did change his personality in line with times and circumstances, his luck would hold steady.* — Machiavelli, The Prince

Your being flexible in the face of obstacles does not make you indecisive. On the contrary. A true leader recognizes when the winds have shifted and a new approach is required.

Your takeaway

James's advice in Thriving at Work was that learning how to do things for yourself like making a Xerox was the key to bigger workplace success.

With Xerox, James meant everything that consists of administrative work. I agree that fortunes rise and fall on the smallest of details, and hence administrative work must be done properly. But I disagree with James that you must do it yourself.

If you want people to think of you as a leader, then you must accomplish two seemingly inconsistent tasks.

- First, appear in all non-substantive things to be utterly helpless, from knowing where coffee comes from to where the lights or air conditioning controls are.

- Second, effortlessly expect that all administrative tasks will be handled by someone around you.

Unless you are alone, in which case your stance on administrative tasks is irrelevant, there is someone around you. Make sure it is them, not you, that jumps to doing little tasks and you will be seen as a leader.

Until next time.

Work well and win.

Chapter Twenty-Five

Take Advantage of Youth, No Matter Your Age

You will have some experienced, old hands. They represent your greatest danger

The young are naïve and manipulable

If there's anything that characterizes young people, it's their lack of interest in history and myopic focus on what's in front of them. This makes them uniquely open to manipulation.

> *Men are more interested in the present than the past and when things are going well they'll be happy and won't look elsewhere.*
> — Machiavelli, The Prince

If it is well-being that engenders unthinking obedience, problems create frustration. In some number of people, problems will get them looking for reasons and solutions. You must ensure that your decisions and actions are never seen as the cause of your team's problems.

Young people make the best ideological zealots

It is easy to frame your team as a bastion of sanity against an uncaring and even adversarial business world. The business would run amok given half a chance, and only the hyper-vigilance of your team stands between shame and success.

Not only that but the leader (you) is investing great personal effort and taking great risks to make sure that the business counterparts understand the stakes and comply.

When you frame the team's work this way, the combination of your efforts and that of your team is like a holy war that requires eternal vigilance. Success is never final, and failure lurks behind each new initiative.

> *If he's sensible the ruler must work out a situation where his citizens will always need both his government and him, however well or badly things are going. Then they will always be loyal.* — Machiavelli, The Prince

When your team trusts you and mistrusts everyone else, you have them in a position where they will carry out your wishes with great fervor.

You want young people on your side

It's unlikely all the employees on your team will be impressionably young. You will have some experienced, old hands. They represent your greatest danger.

They may resent having been passed over and be waiting for a chance to challenge you. And they have seen enough to think independently and challenge your propaganda.

You turn such persons to your advantage by making public examples of them. If they question your message or do not faithfully implement your wishes, you must respond immediately and harshly. A reprimand, a demotion, even a termination. Everyone should see and fear your wrath.

You might fear this would have the team turn against you. Provided you keep your retribution focused and brief, and also lavish rewards and appreciation on those who remain, you will have achieved loyalty that takes years to build organically.

When people are treated well by someone they thought was hostile they respond with even greater loyalty. — Machiavelli, The Prince

Clearing out the older, less easily manipulable team members has several benefits. You eliminate challengers, you free up the budget to hire more young colleagues, and you open up room for internal promotions.

In summary

James's advice in Thriving at Work was that the word Yes is the most important determinant of success at work and in life. He cautions against ever saying No unless the conduct is improper.

One of the greatest myths I've come across is that managers should never say no.

I say this handicaps you from one of the leader's most important tools. Saying no allows you to disrupt or slow down a rival's progress, show displeasure (and indirectly, favor), and ultimately wield power.

Until next time.

Work well and win.

Chapter Twenty-Six

Who Wouldn't Want To Be a Zillionaire?

The only kind of recognition that is objectively measurable and comparable is compensation. Don't let anyone tell you differently

Money motivates everyone

When you have control of a budget, your goal is to spend it wisely. Wisely means first and foremost that you achieve your objectives. Achieving business objectives is usually conducive to your success but is secondary.

One way to help speed your way is to ensure that people in your orbit are handsomely rewarded.

Never scrimp on salaries for your team. Fight to have them be the best paid in the company and across the industry. Whose money are you saving? Shareholders? What have they ever done for you?

> *When the money is his own or his subjects', [the leader] should go easy; when it's someone else's, he should be as lavish as he can.... Spending other people's money doesn't lower your standing, it raises it.* — Machiavelli, The Prince

You will notice your executives having management meetings as often as needed and that they treat themselves well when they meet. There are lessons there for you.

You must treat yourself and your team as befitting the best performers. Do you save a few bucks and alienate your superstars? That is the most foolish kind of penny-pinching. So too your approach to setting expectations for how you and your team should be paid.

Your company should understand that higher pay leads to better performance. This is demonstrably true for lawyers because companies with longer-tenured and hence higher-paid lawyers experience lower total legal costs.

The lower total legal costs presumably come from astute risk management, knowing the business better, and efficient work. But the point to hammer home with the CFO is that it is bad business to lose a lawyer, and hence risky to underpay them.

Nowhere is this truer than for the leader of the team.

Loyalty is another word for sucker

A key lesson about loyalty is that it's something other people have. When your leader is talking about loyalty, it means they're not giving you something you need and deserve, whether resources, support on a project, or pay and promotions.

Seen correctly, loyalty is to be recognized and handsomely rewarded. A leader can trust most the loyalty of the people whose interests are clearly aligned with his own. As in, when their well-being is linked with the leader's well-being.

In contrast, when you are asked to sacrifice for the sake of the company as a whole, for shareholders, or for some other broad group, you can be assured that you are sacrificing for someone else's bonus.

In cases where taking a shared hit is unavoidable, the astute leader will tap pockets of the existing budget to reallocate resources appropriately. You and the team must never suffer for the company's failings.

Performance and money go hand-in-hand

The leader's role is to ensure that their performance and the performance of their allies are well compensated.

Take a thank you and a trophy with humility and grace, but make sure that real performance is backed up by real rewards.

The only kind of recognition that is objectively measurable and comparable is compensation. Don't let anyone tell you differently.

In summary

James's advice in Thriving at Work was that having a Zen-like attitude will bring you both satisfaction and success in work. He notes the benefits of paying careful attention to your thoughts and feelings.

I fully agree that a leader must be keenly attuned to their thoughts and emotions. This allows one to amplify or suppress emotions tactically as the situation warrants.

I say the reward for such control is not peace of mind, but security in an otherwise precarious position of power. It is only by staying in a leadership position that you obtain the full value of the attendant rewards.

This brings my series on the Pragmatist's Rules for Work to an end. I trust you have learned something about how the world works and how you can successfully make your way in it.

I recommend you revisit the series whenever you need inspiration in a tough work situation. We'll be watching and rooting for you.

Work well and win.

www.ingramcontent.com/pod-product-compliance
Lightning Source LLC
Chambersburg PA
CBHW060336050426

42449CB00011B/2769